Hector Macneill

The Links o' Forth

A Parting Peep at the Carse o' Stirling

Hector Macneill

The Links o' Forth
A Parting Peep at the Carse o' Stirling

ISBN/EAN: 9783744673648

Printed in Europe, USA, Canada, Australia, Japan

Cover: Foto ©ninafisch / pixelio.de

More available books at **www.hansebooks.com**

THE LINKS O' FORTH:

OR,

A PARTING PEEP AT THE *CARSE O' STIRLING;*

A PLAINT.

THE

LINKS O' FORTH:

OR, A

PARTING PEEP AT THE *CARSE O' STIRLING;*

A PLAINT.

By HECTOR MACNEIL, Esq.

AUTHOR OF *THE HISTORY O' WILL & JEAN,*
WAES O' WAR, &c.

He woo'd the Muse, and sung the *pensive* strain;
He lov'd meek Solitude, and soften'd gloom;
He caught each link of Fancy's *magic* chain,
And wove the tissue of her airy loom.
STERLING'S CAMBUSCAN. V. 304.

EDINBURGH:

PRINTED FOR ARCHIBALD CONSTABLE, EDINBURGH,
VERNOR AND HOOD, LONDON, AND
BRASH AND REID, GLASGOW.

1799.

THE LINKS O' FORTH:

OR,

A PARTING PEEP AT THE *CARSE O' STIRLING*.

A PLAINT.

— I. —

Ah! winding FORTH!—smooth wandering tide;

O' STREVLIN'S* peerless plain the pride;

How pleas'd alang thy verdant side,

           Whar flowerics spring,

The Muse her untaught numbers tried,

           And learnt to sing!

* The ancient name of Stirling.   B

— 2. —

Whan ardent youth, wi' boiling blood,

Ilk trace o' glowing passion loo'd,

How aft aside thy silver flood,

     Unseen, alane,

The bardie, rapt in pensive mood,

     Has pour'd the strain !

— 3. —

To LAURA, beauteous, mild and young,

His artless lyre he daily strung ;—

Close to his beating heart it hung,

     While glen, and grove,

And craig, and echoing valley, rung

     Wi' fervent love. —

— 4. —

Poor, fond enthusiast! whither stray?

By whimpering burn and broomy brae?

Wasting, I ween, the live-lang day

      In am'rous rhime; —

The hour will come, thou'lt sigh, and say,

      What loss o' time!

— 5. —

Yet, wharfore shou'd nae Youth engage

In pleasures suited to its age?

To catch the tids o' life is sage,

      Some joys to save: —

Wha kens the fights he's doom'd to wage

      This side the grave!

B ij

— 6. —

To sport on *Pleasure*'s flowery brink,

And beek a wee in *Luve*'s warm blink,

Is wiser far, I'm sure, than think

        O' distant harm,

Whan Eild and cauld Indiff'rence shrink

        Frae Pleasure's charm.

— 7. —

Then strike ance mair the trembling lyre;

And, Muse, do thou the sang inspire; —

Ah! check nae yet the glowing fire,

        Tho' Luve divine,

And Youth, and Pleasure's fond desire

        Fast, fast decline!

— 8. —

Attune the lay! whan NATURE's charm

First seiz'd his bosom fluttering warm;

Ere *Care* yet came, wi' rack'd alarm,

    Or *Friendship's guile;*

Or *Fortune*, wi' uplifted arm,

    And treach'rous smile.

— 9. —

Attune the strain that shou'd adorn

Ilk verse descriptive o' the morn;

Whan round FORTH's LINKS o' waving corn,

    At peep o' dawn,

Frae broomy know to whitening thorn,

    He raptured ran;

— 10. —

Or fragrant whar, at opening day,

The whins bloom sweet on OCHIL brae;

There, whan inspired by lofty lay,

            He'd tak his flight;

And towering climb, wi' spirits gay,

            DEMYIT's * height.

— 11. —

Oh! grander far than *Windsor*'s brow!

And sweeter too the vale below!

Whar FORTH's unrivall'd windings flow

            Thro' varied grain,

Brightening, I ween, wi' glittering glow,

            STREVLINA's plain!

* One of the highest of the Ochil hills that bound the Carse of Stirling to the E.

— 12. —

There raptured trace (enthroned on hie)

The landscape stretching on the ee,

Frae Grampian's heights down to the fea,

　　　　　(A dazzling view !)

Corn, villa, hamlet, water, tree,

　　　　　In varying hue. —

— 13. —

Owre lofty here, ilk charm to trace

That decks, sweet plain ! thy cultured face ; —

Aft down the steep he'd tak a race,

　　　　　Nor, rinning, flag,

Till up he'd climb, wi' rapid pace,

　　　　　Yon " *Abbey craig.* "

— 14. —

There seated, mark, wi' ardour keen,

The skelloch * bright 'mang corn sae green;

The purpled pea, and speckled bean;

A fragrant store!

And vessels sailing, morn and e'en,

To " *Stirling shore.* "

— 15. —

But aftner far, he'd, late and ear,

To yonder *castled height* † repair,

Whar Youth's gay sports, relax'd frae care,

Cheat Learning's toils,

And round her DOIG's ‡ classic chair

Fond Genius smiles!

* The wild mustard.
† The castle hill of Stirling, from which the finest view of the Carse is seen.
‡ Dr David Doig, master of the grammar school, which he has taught near 40 years. A man, whose uncommon erudition and genius ought to have entitled to a higher station.

— 16. —

'Twas here, O FORTH! for luve o' thee,

Frae wine, and mirth, and cards he'd flee;

Here too, unskill'd, sweet POESY!

He woo'd thy art —

Alas! nor skill nor guide had he,

Save warmth o' heart!

— 17. —

Yet feckless as his numbers fell,

Nae tongue his peacefu' joys can tell,

Whan, crooning quietly by himsel,

He fram'd the lay,

On GOWLAND's whin-beflowered hill,

And rocky brae,

— 18. —

How richly then the landscape glow'd,

As fast the welcome numbers flow'd!

How smooth the plying bargie row'd

        Frae shore to shore!

How saft the kye in *King's Park* * low'd,

        At milking hour!

— 19. —

And ah! how sweet the murmurs rang

Frae busy Labour's rural thrang!

That sta' the upland heights amang,

        And echoing spread

Owre *Castle*, *Butts*, and *Knott* *, alang

        The *Backwalk* shade!

** See Note A.

— 20. —

Dear, peacefu' scenes ! how sweet to sing !

Whan youth and luve are on the wing ;

Whan morn's fresh gales their fragrance bring,

   Wi' balmy sough,

And e'ening paints (how sweet in Spring !)

   The " braes o' TOUGH!"

— 21. —

But sweet, thro' a' the varying year,

Will AIRTHRIE's banks and woods appear ;

And eke CRAIGFORTH, and princely KEIR,

   That crowns the scene ;

And *Allan water*, glittering near

   Its *Bleaching green.*

— 22. —

And SHAW-PARK, gilt wi' e'ening's ray;

And EMBRO' CASTLE, distant grey; *

Wi' ALVA, sweet by Ochil brae,

'Mang grove and bower

And rich CLACKMANNAN, rising gay,

Wi' woods and tower;

— 23. —

And BLAIR, half hid in silvan shade,

Where *Taste* and *Home* † delighted stray'd;

What time? whan Lear and Genius fled

Frae bar and town,

To TEATH's clear stream, that babbling play'd

By CASTLE DOWN. —

* Edinburgh castle, though distant 35 miles from Stirling, is seen from the castle hill in a favourable day.

† Henry Home, Lord Kames, one of the Senators of the College of Justice, and author of many ingenious and learned performances.

— 24. —

— There, aft he trac'd fond Nature's child!

But maist at e'ening blushing mild,

As owre the western cliffs sae wild

O' LOMOND's * height,

The sun, in setting glory, smil'd

In purple light!

— 25. —

'Twas then, by gloaming's sober hour,

He'd court some solitude obscure;

Or round CAM'SKENNETH's † ancient tower,

Whar winds Forth's stream,

He'd wander, meditate, and pour

This moral theme: —

* Ben Lomond, the highest of the Grampian mountains that bound the Carse of Stirling to the N. W.

† The abbey of Cambuskenneth, founded by David I. King of Scotland, anno 1147.

— 26. —

" How still and solemn steals the gloom,

" Mild owre the garden's fading bloom !

" Dim flits the bat athwart the tomb,

   " On leathern wing ; —

" — Hark ! what bemoan'd the slaughter'd doom

   " O' Scotia's King ? —

— 27. —

" 'Twas but the dove that woo's his mate,

" Regardless of the Monarch's fate : —

" Whar, *Grandeur*, now thy regal state ? —

   " — Unmarkt ! — unknown !

" Nor sculptur'd verse records thy date,

   " Nor moss-grown stone ! "

— 28. —

Yet regal pomp, and courtly show,

Aft graced yon castle's * princely brow,

Whan Scotland's Kings, wi' patriot glow,

             Delighted, woo'd

STREVLINA's fertile fields below,

             And winding flood !

— 29. —

— Sublime retreat ! beloved ! admired !

Whase rural charms sae aft conspired

To calm the raging breast, whan fired

             'Gainst lawless power,

And yield, mid social sweets retired,

             Life's happier hour !

* See Note E.

— 30. —

To sheath in peace War's slaughtering sword;

To drap the *King* at *Friendship*'s board;

To draw frae Luve's delicious hoard

      Her honey'd sweet!

And chain fierce Valour's lofty lord

     At *Beauty*'s feet.

— 31. —

Or join the chace, at purple morn,

Owre lawns, and heath-bloom'd mountains borne;

Wi' hounds, and hawks, and bugle horn,

      And fhouting thrang;

While SAUCHIE's dales, beflower'd wi' thorn,

      The notes prolang;

— 32. —

Or break the lance, and couch the spear,

At *tilts* and *tournaments* o' weir,

Whar mony a valiant knight and peer

          Display'd their skill,

To courtly beauty, brightening near,

          On LADY's HILL *.

— 33. —

—Thus tun'd to Pastime's peacefu' string,

Strevlina's craigs and valley * ring ;

Blythe roam'd the Courtier and his King

          Round *Fortha*'s flood,

Till *Faction* soar'd on raven wing,

          Bedrapt wi' blood !

** See Note C.   C

— 34· —

'Twas then ilk sport and rural charm

Fled court, and plain, and joyless farm !—

Rebellion dire, wi' dread alarm,

          Shriek'd madd'ning by,

And *Murder* dark, wi' dagger'd arm

          And blood-shot eye !

— 35· —

O *Treason !*—ranc'rous, ruthless foe !

Sad source o' *Scotland*'s wars and woe !

Not guiltless grandeur, here laid low *,

          Could calm thy strife,

Nor ward thy deadly, dastard blow,

          And butchering knife !

* James III, murdered in the village of Bannockburn, after the battle fought with his rebellious nobles, under the command of the Duke of Rothsay, his own son. He was buried near the remains of his Queen, in the abbey church of Cambuskenneth, 1488.

— 36. —

Alas! nor HE *, whase youthfu' bloom

Lang felt Oppression's tyrant doom ;

Tho' *Science*, mid the captive gloom,

            And *Genius* bright,

And *Fancy*, at her fairy loom,

            Shot radiant light !—

— 37. —

—Insatiate fiend! could nought allay

The rebel rage 'gainst Regal sway !—

Not FLODDEN-FIELD, whase fatal day

            Brought dool and care,

Whan Scotland's *Flowers* ware wed away †,

            To bloom nae mair.

C ij

* James I. of Scotland. See note D.
† Alluding to the beautiful and pathetic ballad of the " Flowers of the
" Foreſt."

— 38. —

Nor Esk's death heart-break, and disgrace *,

Nor Mary's † tears, nor beauteous face,

Could stop, fell fae! thy infuriate pace,

    Bestain'd wi' crime,

Till *Stuart*'s royal, luckless race!

    Fled *Scotia*'s clime.

— 39. —

—Dark lower'd the morn, wi' aspect drie,

Whan *Scotia*, sad, wi' tearfu' ee,

Saw, frae her pine-wav'd cliffs on hie,

    And aiken bowers,

Her King, and Independence flee

    Strevlina's towers!

* James V. was so affected with the unfortunate and disgraceful affair of Solway Frith, that he died a very few days afterwards, literally of a broken heart.
† Mary Queen of Scots.

— 40. —

Not sae the morn, that beaming shed

A blaze round WALLACE' helmed head,

As bald in Freedom's cause he led

His patriot train,

And dyed these blood-drench'd furrows red

Wi' hostile slain !

— 41. —

" Nor yet, O BRUCE * ! the morn that shone

Bright, bright! whan (EDWARD's host ow'rthrown)

High, on yon proud hill's *standard stone* †,

Thy banners flew ;

While *Freedom*, loud, in raptured tone,

Her clarion blew !

C iij

* King Robert the Bruce.

† The stone where Bruce's standard was fixed during the memorable battle of Bannockburn. It may still be seen on an eminence near the village of St Ninians, with a hole in the centre where the end of the standard was fixed, and

— 42. —

" —Enchanting morn! whase magic reign

Brake forging Thraldom's galling chain;

Led CERES, wi' her laughing train

And golden store,

Round BANNOCKBURN's ensanguin'd plain,

And CARRON's shore,

— 43. —

" Round *Carun's stream*, o' classic name,

Whar FINGAL fought, and ay ow'rcame *;

Whar OSSIAN wak'd, wi' kindling flame,

His heav'n-taught lays,

And sang his OSCAR's deathless fame

At *Dunipace !* *

*⁊ See Note F.

— 44. —

" —*Names*, gratefu' to the Patriot's ear !

Which SCOTIA's sons delight to hear !—

Names, that the Brave will lang revere

     Wi' valour's sigh !

—Dear to the Muse !—but doubly dear

     To LIBERTY ! "

— 45. —

Thus (blind to Prudence' warning light)

Aft sigh'd and sang the pensive wight !—

Reckless, alas ! o' *Fortune*'s blight,

     And *warldly blame*,

He'd muse, and dream, till dark midnight,

     Then daunder hame !

— 46. —

—Ye classic *Plains*, and winding *Stream !*

Ye stately *Towers !* whar morn's first beam,

Mild glittering, gilds with golden gleam !

—'Twas *yours* the crime!

—'Twas YE first tempt' his youth to dream

In thriftless rhime !

— 47. —

'Twas *ye* first taught him to despise

The oil of FLATTERY's false disguise,

And all the winding wiles that rise

To wealth and state ;

And told him still bold TRUTH to prize,

Unaw'd by fate.

— 48. —

'Twas *ye* first learnt him to explore

The charms of NATURE's boundless store!

Whether he gaz'd her beauties o'er

      On Britain's isle;

Or caught them on some foreign shore,

      With softer smile!

— 49. —

Whether (by wayward fortune tost!)

He found her, where he woo'd her most,

On bland JANEIRO's * heav'nly coast

      And balmy clime,

Where oft the *Beautiful* is lost

      In the *Sublime :*

* Rio de Janeiro, capital of the Brazils.

— 50. —

Whether, in curling mist survey'd,

On Afric's storm-beat Cape * she stay'd;

Or, bright in all her charms array'd,

In Ceylon's vale,

From blossom'd bank and spicy glade,

Perfum'd the gale;

— 51. —

Or westward, where, with dimpling smiles,

She greets *Charibia*'s palm-girt isles,

With glowing cheek, and winning wiles,

Each breast to move,

And e'en the gloom of Slavery's toils

Lights into love !

* The Cape of Good Hope.

— 52. —

—Whether to either India borne,

(Or flush'd with hope, or woe—forlorn)

He hail'd her balmy breath at morn

> From *Orange flower*,

Or Cassia bud, or *Logwood thorn*,

> Or *Guava bower* ;

— 53. —

Or from the mountain's misty brow,

Enhal'd the spicy gales that blow

Fresh from *Pimento*'s * groves below,

> That gild the scene ;

Crown'd with their whitening flowers that glow

> Thro' deepening green !

* See Note G.

— 54· —

—Whether at noon, recumbent laid,

He woo'd the dear enticing maid,

Under the *Banyan*'s pillar'd shade *

                On plain or hill,

Or *Plantain* green, that, rustling, play'd

                Across the rill ;

— 55· —

Or from the *Tam'rind*'s glimmering gloom,

Drank coolnefs, wafted by perfume,

From lime, or Shaddach's golden bloom ;

                While, fluttering gay,

Humm'd soft the bird of peerless plume †,

                From spray to spray !

* See Note H.
† See Note I.

— 56. —

—Whether at eve, with glowing breast,

The whitening, palm-deck'd beach he prest,

And eyed, entranc'd, the purpling west

                  Bepictur'd o'er *,

As ocean, softly murmuring, kist

                    The shelving shore :

— 57. —

Or, by the moon's bright radiance led,

Roam'd lone the Guinea-verdur'd glade ‡,

Where towers the giant *Ceiba*'s shade † ;

                  And, loftier still,

The *Cabbage* ‖ rears its beauteous head

                  O'er grove and hill :

* See Note K.   † See Note L.

‡ Guinea grass pasture; See Edwards's hist. 8vo, vol. I. p. 186.

‖ The Palmeto Royal, or *mountain cabbage*, from 150 to 200 feet in height ; " a tree which, without doubt," says Mr Edwards, " is among the most grace- " ful of all the vegetable creation."

— 58. —

Or, rapt at twilight, glimmering grey,

(As gleam'd the *fin-fly*'s myriad ray *),

Thro' groves where harmless lightnings play,

> He humm'd along ;

To NATURE pour'd, in fervent lay,

> The Muse's song.

— 59. —

Yet, as he felt her magic charms,

And woo'd her to his ardent arms ;

Oft, mindful of her fond alarms

> On STREVLIN's plain,

He thought on all her *witching harms* !

> And checkt the strain :

* See Note M.

— 60. —

And, as he mus'd each rapture o'er,

That warm'd on FORTHA's winding ſhore;

His heart, with rack'd remembrance sore,

    Sad, sorrowing bled;

While scenes, that brightening beam'd before—

    In darkness—fled!

THE END.

A. " Upon the south west of the Castle, lies a large park,
    " inclosed with a stone wall, called the *King's Park,*
    " where the Court used to divert themselves with hunt-
    " ing of the deer, which were kept in it.   At the east
    " end of the Park lie the Royal Gardens : vestiges of
    " the walks and parterres, with a few stumps of fruit
    " trees, are still visible.—In the gardens is a mound of
    " earth, in form of a table, called the *King's Knott,*
    " with benches of earth round it, where, according to
    " tradition, the Court sometimes held *fêtes champêtres.*
    " Around the gardens, too, are vestiges of a canal, upon
    " which the Royal Family and Court used to divert
    " themselves in pleasure boats. "

                       Nimmo's Hist. of Stirlingshire, p. 250, 251.

B. The Castle of Stirling, on account of its beautiful situ-
    ation and delightful prospect, was the favourite residence
    of our Scotish Kings, particularly of the James's. —
    James III. was so attached to it, that he built a palace,
    with an elegant chapel in it. — To procure funds for the
    support of a dean, prebends, a numerous band of sing-
    ers, musicians, and other officers, he suppressed the
    Priory of Coldingham, and endowed his chapel with the
                                                  revenues:

revenues : a circumstance which produced the rebellion
that shortly after occasioned the tragical death of that
mild and unfortunate monarch. — *See Henry's Hist. of
Great Britain.*

C. " In the Castle hill, is a hollow, called the *Valley*, com-,
" prehending about an acre of ground, and having all the
" appearance of an artificial work, which was used for
" tilts and tournaments, with other feats of chivalry;
" and closely adjoining to this valley upon the south, is
" a small rocky mount, rising in form of a pyramid,
" called the *Lady's Hill*, upon which the Ladies of the
" Court took their station to behold those exercises."
Nimmo's Hist. p. 252.

D. " James I. of Scotland was one of the most accomplish-
" ed and amiable princes that ever filled a throne. He
" was likewise one of the most unfortunate. After up-
" wards of 18 years captivity in England, and encoun-
" tering many difficulties on his return to his native
" kingdom, he was, in the prime of life, murdered by
" barbarous assassins in the Carthusian monastery of
" Perth. In the monument of genius, James has been
" almost equally unfortunate. No vestiges are now re-
" maining of his skill in *architecture, gardening,* and
" *painting,* though we are well assured, by one who
" was well acquainted with him *, that in all thefe arts
" he excelled. Many of the productions of his pen have
" also perished; for he tells us himself † that he *wrote*

" *much;*

* Scotichron. lib. 16. cap. 30.

† King's Quair, cant. 1. stan. 13.

" *much;* and we know of only three of his poems that
" are now extant, viz. *Christ's Kirk on the Green, Peebles*
" *to the Play,* and the *King's Quair,* which was lately
" discovered by Mr Warton, and since published by
" William Tytler of Woodhouselee, Esq." *Henry's Hist.*
" He was (continues Henry) not only the most learned
" King, but one of the most learned men of the age in
" which he flourished; and seems to have been born to
" excel in every art to which he applied his mind."—
Independently of his other singular accomplishments, he
particularly excelled in *music,* not only as a performer,
but as a *composer;* and it is to his admirable genius,
that the musical world is so much indebted for the in-
vention (amidst the gloom of solitude and confinement)
of that sweet and plaintive Scotch and Italian * melody,
which, as the above mentioned author justly remarks,
" has given pleasure to millions in every succeeding
" age."

E.—F. " Raise, ye bards of the song, (said Fingal) the wars
" of the *streamy Carun.* CARACUL has fled from my
" arms,

* *Alexandero Tassoni* mentions James King of Scotland, having, of himself, in-
vented a *new kind of music,* plaintive and melancholy, different from all others,
in which he was imitated by Carlo Gesualdo, prince of Venosa, who, in our age,
(says Passoni) has improved music with new and admirable inventions. As the
Prince of Venosa *imitated King James,* the other musicians of *Italy* imitated the
Prince of Venosa. " The most noble Carlo Gesualdo, the prince of musicians in
" our age, (says Sir John Hawkins, vol. 3. p. 212.) introduced such a style of
" modulation, that other musicians yield the preference to him; and all singers
" and players on stringed instruments, laying aside that of others, every where
embraced his."

" arms, along the fields of his pride. He sets far dis-
" tant, like a meteor that encloses a spirit of night,
" when the winds drive it over the heath, and the dark
" woods are gleaming around."—" What does CAROS
" King of Ships, said the son of the now mournful
" Ossian? Spreads he the wings of his pride, bard of
" the times of old ?—He spreads them, Oscar, replied
" the bard; but it is behind his *gathered heap*; he looks
" over his stones with fear, and beholds thee terrible as
" the ghost of night, that rolls the wave to his ships."
See the *War of Caros*, and the beautiful poem *Comala*.

C. " The pimento trees grow spontaneously, and in great
" abundance, in many parts of Jamaica, but more par-
" ticularly on hilly situations near the sea, on the north-
" ern side of the island, where they form the most deli-
" cious groves that can possibly be imagined, filling the
" air with fragrance, and giving reality, though in a
" very distant part of the globe, to our great poet's de-
" scription of those balmy gales which convey to the de-
" lighted voyager

" Sabean odours from the spicy shore
" Of Araby the blest.
" Cheer'd with the grateful smell, old ocean smiles."
" I do not believe that there is in all the vegetable crea-
" tion, a tree of greater beauty than a young pimento.
" The trunk, which is of a grey colour, smooth and
" shining, and altogether free of bark, rises to the
" height of fifteen or twenty feet. It then branches out
" on all sides, richly clothed with leaves of a deep
" green,

" green, somewhat like those of the bay tree ; and these,
" in the months of July and August, are beautifully
" contrasted and relieved by an exuberance of white
" flowers. It is remarkable, that the leaves are equally
" fragrant with the fruit; and, I am told, yield in dis-
" tillation a delicate odoriferous oil, which is very com-
" monly used in the medical dispensaries of Europe for
" oil of cloves." *Edwards's hist. of the West Indies,*
8vo, *vol.* 2. *p.* 297.

H. " This monarch of the woods," (says Mr Edwards, in
his elegant history), " whose empire extends over Asia
" and Africa, as well as the tropical parts of America, is
" described by our divine poet with great exactness.

" The *fig-tree,* not that kind for fruit renown'd,
" But such as at this day to Indians known
" In Malabar and Decan ; spreads his arms,
" Branching so broad and long, that in the ground
" The bearded twigs take root, and daughters grow
" Above the mother tree ; *a pillar'd shade*
" *High over-arch'd, and echoing walks between.*"

Paradise Lost, book 9.

It is called in the East Indies, the *banyan tree.* Mr Mars-
den gives the following account of the dimensions of one
near Mangee, twenty miles west of Patna in Bengal.
Diameter, 363 to 375 feet; circumference of the shadow
at noon, 1116 feet; circumference of the several stems,
in number fifty or sixty, 921 feet.

Hist. Sumatra, p. 131.

I. " The humming bird, the most beautiful, as well as the
    " most diminutive, of the feathered race, is fond of
    " building its nest in the *tamarind*, orange, or bastard
    " cedar-trees; on account, I should suppose, of the su-
    " perabundance of their shade. The nest is made with
    " particular art and beauty. The workmanship, indeed,
    " is no less exquisite than wonderful, and seems to be,
    " in an essential manner, adapted as the residence of
    " this interesting and lovely bird." *Beckford's descriptive*
    account of the island of Jamaica.—For a more particular de-
    scription, see *vol.* 1. *p.* 363, 8*vo edit. of the same work.*

K. The following very animated, though inflated description
    of a tropical sky at sunset, is taken from the same au-
    thor :—" Of the picturesque representation of the clouds
    " in Jamaica, there is an almost daily and unspeakable
    " variety; and the sunset of that climate has charms to
    " arrest the regard, and fix the attention, of every be-
    " holder. At this period, when the sun-beams linger
    " on the mountains, and seem reluctantly to withdraw
    " their glories from the plain; when they just begin to
    " die away in the horizon, or glitter by reflexion upon
    " the trembling wave ;—what delightful appearances, or
    " glowing with lustre, or softened by shade, may not
    " be imagined or lamented in the evanescent clouds of
    " that warm and vapoury region! What imaginary
    " islands, with all the discriminations of hill and dale,
    " of light and gloom, of bays and promontories, of
    " rocks and woods, of rivers and seas, may not be traced
    " in the transcendently beautiful skies of that fervent
                                        " climate,

" climate, and treasured up for future embellishments,
" by those who study nature, and who delight to copy
" her charms, not only in her elevation, but decline !"

Vol. I. *p.* 80.

L. What European forest has ever given birth to a stem e-
qual to that of the Ceiba, *(or wild cotton-tree)*, which a-
lone, simply rendered concave, has been known to pro-
duce a boat capable of containing one hundred persons ?

Edwards's hist. vol. I. *p.* 15.

M. In the mountainous and interior parts of the larger
islands, innumerable *fin-flies* abound at night, which have
a surprising appearance to a stranger. They consist of
different species, some of which emit a light, resembling
a spark of fire, from a globular prominence near each
eye ; and others from their sides, in the act of respira-
tion. They are far more luminous than the glow-worm,
and fill the air on all sides, like so many living stars, to
the great astonishment of a traveller unaccustomed to
the country. In the day-time they disappear.

Edwards's hist. vol. I. *p.* 8.

LATELY PUBLISHED, AND TO BE HAD OF

ARCHIBALD CONSTABLE, EDINBURGH,

———

1. SCOTLAND's SKAITH; or, HISTORY O' WILL and JEAN, owre true a Tale; with some Additional Poems, by Hector Macneil Esquire, *embellished with engravings.* Price 3s. 6d.

2. THE WAES O' WAR; or, The Upshot o' the History o' Will and Jean. Price 1s.

3. EPISTLE from Lady GRANGE to EDWARD D——— Esquire, written during her confinement in the island of St Kilda, *the second edition.* Price 2s.

4. PICTURES of POETRY, historical, biographical, and critical, by Alexander Thomson Esq. Price 5s.

5. The PLEASURES of HOPE, by Thomas Campbell. Price 6s.

IN THE PRESS,

SCOTISH POEMS, of the SIXTEENTH CENTURY,

www.ingramcontent.com/pod-product-compliance
Lightning Source LLC
Chambersburg PA
CBHW032136080426
42733CB00008B/1092